Contents

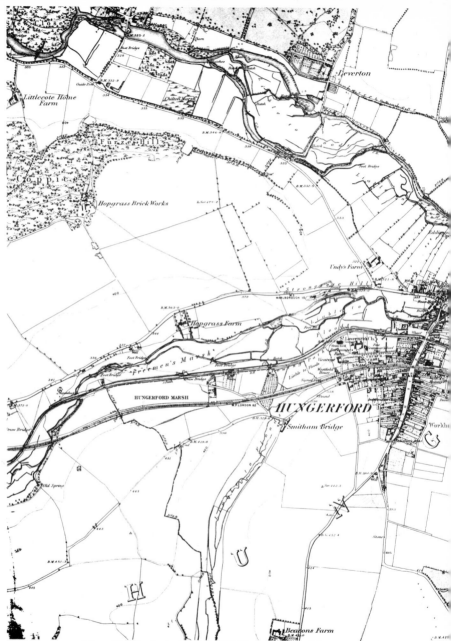

Ordnance Survey Map – 6″ to 1 mile. 1st Edition 1882: The expansion of the town over the last 100 years is evident from this map.

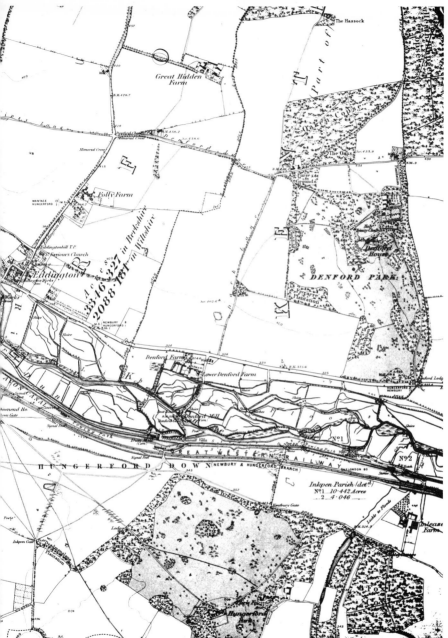

Notice how The Priory then lay in open country, although now it stands amongst houses, with the John of Gaunt School opposite.

Preface

'Oh yes, I know Hungerford. We used to go through it on the way to Bath. Of course we don't now that the M4's open, but I remember it well. We stopped sometimes at that nice old hotel – was it called The Bear?'

Such a conversation will be very familiar to all Hungerford residents, often with 'It must be an interesting old town' added as an afterthought. But in travelling through on the Bath Road, little of the town itself is seen. A turning just by The Bear takes you across the old canal bridge, and under the railway. The road opens out then into one of those broad High Streets so often seen in country market towns, lined on both sides by shops and houses – many still displaying their fine seventeenth and eighteenth century frontages.

An interesting old town it is – both to its residents and to the increasing number of visitors who pause a while here on their journey.

This book makes no attempt to be an exhaustive history of Hungerford. For that more scholarship, more time, and more space are required. It does, however, outline the key events in the development of this much-loved town, and of the community it supports.

The Origins of the Town

The modern town of Hungerford lies on the southern slopes of the Kennet Valley. This river plays an important part in the history of the town, and has been famous for centuries for its fine trout fishing. It originates from springs high up on the chalk downlands of Wiltshire, and these downs, along with those of Berkshire and Hampshire, lay at the very centre of Britain's earliest inhabitation – by Stone Age man.

He found the chalk downs excellently suited to his needs, and within 15 miles of Hungerford are some of the greatest relics of the Stone Age (before 2500 BC) – the largest stone circle in Britain is at Avebury; the largest man-made hill in Europe at Silbury; the longest Neolithic long barrow at West Kennet; the oldest long barrow in Britain is at Lambourn; and the oldest carved hill figure is at Uffington. On the high ridge of the Downs a few miles south of Hungerford is the Combe long barrow – at a position commanding fine and extensive views across the Kennet Valley to the Lambourn Downs 20 miles to the north. All these reflect the importance of the area during the Stone Age period.

As tools improved and farming skills developed, so successive cultures gradually began to descend from the downs and cultivate the densely wooded valley. The earliest Bronze Age cultures (c. 2000 BC) were the Beaker people, so-named because of their distinctive drinking vessels. A very large and well-preserved beaker, 29 cms high, was found at Inkpen some years ago, and is on display at Newbury Museum.

Other relics of the Bronze Age have been found at Leverton, and at Denford, which appears to have been the site of a ford over the Kennet from at least 1400 BC.

At the very summit of Inkpen Hill, just east of the Combe long barrow, is the extensive Iron Age hill camp of Walbury. Indeed, enclosing an area of 82 acres, Walbury is one of the largest hill forts in the country. Within a 12 mile radius of Hungerford, however, there are a further 14 examples, indicating a comparatively large population around 500 BC.

Some centuries later, after further invasions by the Belgae, of Celtic and Germanic stock, the great Roman empire under Claudius expanded across the English Channel in AD 43 and overran southern Britain. Such was the organization of the Romans that very quickly military bases were established across the country, joined by fine-quality roads. Within a few years, most of the southern part of Britain was living a reasonably peaceful life under Roman rule. Many of the more important roads are distinguishable today.

A road from the area capital of Calleva Atrebatum (Silchester) passed west and slightly north, crossing the Kennet at a ford near Thatcham. It passed on just north of Newbury to the military station of Spinae (Speen), and then north-west towards Durocornovium (Wanborough) and Corinium (Cirencester). This road is today called Ermine Street, going through Wickham, Shefford Woodlands, and Baydon. A branch off the road at Wickham, took a westerly route towards Aquae Sulis (Bath). Its line can still be traced passing Orpenham Farm, Clapton and Radley, to the junction of Wantage Road with Gipsy Lane (Folly Crossing) just north of Hungerford. From here its exact position is not clear, but it continued its westerly course, fording the river between Hungerford and Chilton Foliat, and then ran on the southern bank until it reached the military station of Cunetio (Mildenhall), where several roads met.

At Littlecote Park, a mile to the west of Hungerford, recent excavations have rediscovered the famous Orpheus mosaic, which was originally found in 1730, but covered soon after by the owner of the estate to avoid publicity. The mosaic, which is itself very unusual in this part of the Roman Empire, lies in an elaborate chamber at the end of one wing of an extensive Roman building. The Orpheus Room was clearly connected with a religious sect, and dates from the later period of Roman occupation, but the full story of this interesting and important set of buildings will only unfold as the excavations proceed.

The Roman occupation of Britain lasted nearly four hundred years. During the fourth century there were repeated incursions by the Picts and Scots, as well as invasions from across the Channel by the Saxons. In 406 the Roman troops in Britain were transferred back to the continent, and by 410 the withdrawal was complete. The occupation had lasted the equivalent of 12 generations – the same span of time from Queen Elizabeth I to the present day. Despite this, the Britons themselves appear to have learned little about government and organization. Appeals went to Rome for reconsideration of the evacuation, but the empire was collapsing, there were greater problems elsewhere, and the last appeal dated 446 was ignored like the others before. British history drifted reluctantly into the period known as the Dark Ages, although recent knowledge and research is shedding some light upon it.

The area around Hungerford is full of names with Saxon origins. Only the major features, such as the rivers (Kennet, Dun, Inge), bear signs of Celtic derivation. The table below shows some examples:

-ton)	Enclosed group of cottages	Eddington, Chilton, Leverton,
-ham)		Clapton, Templeton, Ham,
		Wickham.
-dene	Chalky valley	Standen, Hidden, Pidden.
-bourne	Brook or stream	Lambourn, Aldbourne,
		Shalbourne.
-burh	Hill-fort	Kintbury, Walbury, Ramsbury,
		Membury, Fosbury.
-ley	Pasture	Radley, Soley, Poughley.
-cote	Stone enclosure	Littlecote, Elcot, Wawcott.

Hungerford lay in the area occupied by the West Saxons and the most famous of the Wessex kings, indeed one of the greatest rulers of all time, was Alfred, born at Wantage in about 848. He ascended the throne in 871, and led his forces in many famous battles to stem the advance of the Danish settlers. It was at the Wiltshire Eddington in 878 that he finally routed the Danes, but Alfred owned the Eddington near Hungerford, and it passed to his wife on his death in 901.

It is to this period that one account of the origin of the name Hungerford is ascribed. An ancient book entitled the *Book of Hyde* recounts the story of the struggle between the Danes and Saxons, and it mentions a Danish leader named Hingwar, who 'was drowned as he was crossing a morass in Berkshire, which morass is called to this day by the people of that country Hyngerford'. This rather romantic explanation is generally discounted, however, not having been written until about 500 years after the supposed event!

The more prosaic interpretation is of a ford leading to a place of hunger, or poverty. This suggestion, whilst undoubtedly the more correct, has less attraction to local people!

In 1066 Duke William of Normandy conquered England. He was crowned King, and within very few years most of the lands of the English nobility had been granted to his Norman followers. The Saxon Chronicle records that in 1085 'at Gloucester at mid-winter, the King sent men all over England to find out what or how much land each landowner held, and what it was worth'. This great Domesday Survey was very thorough, and has provided the modern historian with a detailed account of even the smallest hamlet, often forming the foundation stone of a local history.

For Hungerford, however, there is no record. This simple statement of fact is at first sight rather surprising. The whole area around Hungerford was part of the Hundred of Cheneteberie or Kintbury. Eddington is mentioned, with its 300 acres and a mill, as is Leverton – with over 500 acres and a mill. Two manors in Inkpen are detailed, along with Denford, Avington, and Inglewood. Whilst there are several possible explanations for the absence of a Hungerford entry, it is probable that the land in the area was owned by the King as Royal Forest, and that any hamlet was of insufficient size or importance to have justified a separate entry.

Despite this disappointment, it was not long before the name of Hungerford appeared in print. In 1108 there is a record of the church at Hungerford being assigned along with the manor of Eddington to the Norman Abbey of Bec Helloin. In 1147 the church is mentioned again, when the Priory of St Frideswide's at Oxford exchanged the church of Beaumont in Normandy for the 'manor of Hudden and the vill of Edineton', one third of the tithings to be reserved for the church at Hungerford on the understanding that no church or chapel be built at Eddington. The nearby manor of Avington had a Norman church, and this building still stands today near the manor house, one of the finest and unaltered Norman chapels in the country.

In the 1170's the men of Hungerford had the right of *firma burgi*, and possessed a common seal for official use, showing that by this time a responsible and well-organized community had developed here, a fact which will be referred to in a later chapter.

Visitors to Hungerford will often stand in the High Street, and look in vain for the church. Unusually, it is some way from the centre of the town, to the west, on the other side of the green area known as The Croft. This church of St Lawrence is the third church on the site, and its Norman predecessor would have stood here nearly 900 years ago. The early village would have clustered around it, spilling on to The Croft and the southern part of Freeman's Marsh.

Around the end of the twelfth century, it would appear that for some reason the old village was becoming unsatisfactory for further expansion. Perhaps it was too wet, lying as it did so close to the marsh, or perhaps the owners of the manor had the foresight to see the advantage to themselves of planning a completely new town, a few hundred yards to the east, where the natural contour of the land provided an obvious setting. Around this time many towns benefitted by Royal Charters, and although there is no suggestion of a charter for Hungerford, the surge of new town building may have influenced the planning of new Hungerford.

This plan consisted of strips of burgage plots about 100 yards long, for a 450 yard length along both sides of the north–south main street. The mediaeval plough teams tended to form a shallow S-shaped furrow to facilitate the turning of the oxen at the end of each drive, and the pronounced bend in the property boundaries, especially those to the west of the High Street, suggests that the burgage plots were laid out on the strips of the open fields of the earlier settlement by the church. This bend can easily be seen when standing in the High Street, and looking along Church Lane, the little passage running through to The Croft. The back lanes behind the

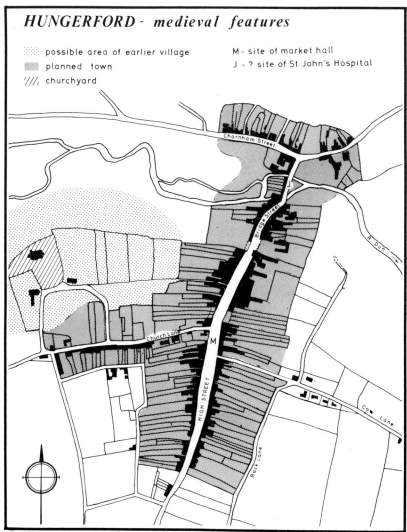

HUNGERFORD - medieval features

:::::: possible area of earlier village   M - site of market hall

▓▓ planned town   J - ? site of St John's Hospital

//// churchyard

Medieval Features: The stippled area around the church is the probable site of the early village. The medieval town laid out during the twelfth century is shown in grey. Strictly speaking, the northern limit of the town was at the Priory (or Hospital) of St John (marked J on the plan). Charnham Street was a separate manor until 1894.

burgage plots survive today as Fairview Road on the east and Prospect Road on the west.

Throughout the thirteenth century, Hungerford grew in size and prosperity. In 1241 it was called a borough for the first time, and in 1284 it was referred to as 'Hungerford Regis' – emphasizing it as an ancient demesne of the Crown. A charter of 1296–7 mentions its market, and there were two watermills in addition to the one at Eddington mentioned in Domesday. By 1361 a fair was established, increasing the town's importance as a 'rural community' (as it had been designated in a tax document of 1334).

Between 1348 and 1350 the whole of the country was afflicted by the dreadful epidemic of bubonic plague; the 'Black Death' is estimated to have caused the death of no less than half of the population, and there is no reason to suppose that Hungerford fared any better than average. It may be this terrible loss of life that led to the failure to develop all the burgage plots which had been laid out during the previous century. Rocques map of 1761, and the Enclosure Award map of 1819 both suggest that the planned development extended as far as the modern Tarrants Hill and Atherton Road, although large areas were unused.

In the mid-fourteenth century, therefore, Hungerford was a small but expanding village, based on the twelfth-century layout. In addition to the market and fair, the local watermills brought trade to the town, although the Black Death had no doubt set back its development. This then is the town which existed at the time of John of Gaunt.

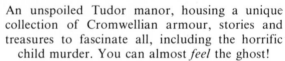

John of Gaunt, The Trustees, and Hocktide

From the time of the Domesday Book, the lands of Hungerford, along with those of Kintbury had passed through a succession of Norman lessees. One, Robert de Beaumont, was created First Earl of Leicester in 1102, and so began a long association between the manor and the House of Leicester. Much later, in 1232, the estate passed to Simon de Montfort, founder of our modern parliament. At this time some of the parish, about 500 acres in the south and west on the sandy down, was held by William de Breteignoll, as a knights fee for feudal service. The association of this area of 'Sanden Fee' has always been close, indeed the church itself stands on land 'in the Fee'.

During the early fourteenth century, the estate passed frequently between the Crown and the Duchy of Leicester, and by this time it was usual for the Earls of Leicester also to be Earls of Lancaster. Indeed, this was the situation when Henry, who had been made Earl of Leicester on his father's death in 1345, was created Duke of Lancaster in 1351. Henry married Isabel of Beaumont, but died in 1361, leaving no sons but two daughters, Maud and Blanche. Maud inherited the estates, but she died childless on 10th April, 1362, and the manor of Hungerford, along with many other estates, passed to her younger sister Blanche, wife of Edward III's fourth son, John of Gaunt. This date is therefore of some interest to Hungerfordians.

John of Gaunt was born in 1340, and was aged 22 years when his sister-in-law Maud died. With Blanche he had three children, but Blanche herself died in 1369, shortly after the birth of their younger daughter. John soon married again, and later, by his third wife, Katherine Swynford, he had four more children. Whilst it was John's son by his first marriage, Henry Bolingbroke – later Henry IV, who started the Wars of the Roses, it was a descendant of his youngest daughter by his marriage to Katherine, namely Elizabeth of York, who was eventually to seal the end of the Wars, when she married the Lancastrian King Henry VII.

Many traditions surround Hungerford's association with John of Gaunt. Chief amongst them is that it was John himself who granted the inhabitants of the town the right to fish in the River Kennet, from Eldren Stubb (on the river just below Leverton) as far as Irish Stile (at least two miles below Kintbury). To support this tradition, there is in the town's possession an ancient (and battered!) brass horn, which is said to have been given to the town by John of Gaunt, as guarantee of those rights. The horn has the word 'Hungerford' on one side, and on the other is a partially defaced word 'Actel' or 'Astel', along with the badge of the Crescent and Star, now recognized as the Arms of Hungerford.

It is said that there was a written charter confirming those rights, but that the Duchy copy was lost in the fire at John of Gaunt's Savoy Palace in The Strand during the riots of 1381, and that the town's copy was allegedly stolen in the days of Queen Elizabeth I. A detailed account of the events surrounding the trial in 1573 of the two men charged with the theft is given in the Reverend Summers book *Story of Hungerford.* In summary, however, the court found that the burgesses of Hungerford were not a 'Corporation' sufficient to plead; that there was no proof of the removal of the documents from the town chest; and that even if documents had been taken, there was no proof that the town had suffered any loss as a result!

In the developing struggle between the Duchy and the burgesses of Hungerford, this 'Charters Case' encouraged the Duchy officials to attempt to regain control of the fishery, or at least to get some payment for it. If there was no charter proclaiming the right of free fishing, then the Duchy were going to try hard to prevent the apparent 'poaching' of its waters. For their part, the residents of Hungerford, having enjoyed free fishing for generations, were not going to give up the benefit lightly.

This strength of feeling may seem rather out of proportion to a generation who now in the 1980's fish the rivers largely as a recreation. But in the Middle Ages eating fish was an important part of the diet, a good source of protein throughout the year, and especially welcome during the late winter when the only meat available would have been salted during the autumn. Following the Reformation, the former fish-eating day of Friday became compulsory, with the addition of Saturday, and in 1563, Wednesday. The growing importance of fish made the right of free fishing especially valuable. A 'battle royal' commenced!

An appeal was made by the burgesses to Queen Elizabeth when she was staying at Salisbury with the Earl of Pembroke, who was High Steward of Hungerford. She replied, in the now famous letter, on 7th September, 1574, confirming 'that the said inhabitants should hereafter have use and enjoy without interruption all such liberties and profits and benefits as heretofore time out of mind and remembrance of man they had used and enjoyed'. This royal reply might appear at first a true shot in the arm for the townsmen, but note that at no stage did it actually spell out any specific right. It was, in effect, a very diplomatic document; the Queen clearly did not wish to get too involved in the struggle between the Duchy and some of its tenants!

For the next 40 years or so, a succession of legal wrangles, inquiries, and surveys was carried out, and there are good accounts both in Summers'

Story of Hungerford and Davis' *The Story of an Ancient Fishery*.

Eventually, in 1611, the Duchy set up yet another commission to inquire into the history of the 'Kynnett, commonly called the Hungerford Brook, famous above all rivers thereabouts for good trout, which fishery had been impaired by lewd and ill-disposed persons fishing unlawfully'. Of the many concluding statements, the following were perhaps the crux:

1. The fishing extended from Elder Stubb to Irish Stile;
2. The King (James I) was Lord Royal of all water except the mill pounds;
3. The townsmen of Hungerford had had the right of fishing in the waters, three days a week, time out of mind.

The inquiry had to a large extent gone against the townsfolk, and it signalled an end to the 'John of Gaunt' era of heresay rights. In the future, Hungerford was going to have its rights secured on a legal and recognized basis. As they were not a corporation, the townspeople decided to proceed by means of feoffees, or trustees.

In March 1612, James I duly granted the Manor of Hungerford with all manorial rights to two London men, John Eldred and William Whitmore, and in May, 'in consideration of a certain sum of money', Eldred and Whitmore conveyed the Manor, complete with 'rents, pleas, perquisites of court of burgh, with fishery and fishing of all rivers and waters in the manor aforesaid' to four Hungerford men. John Lucas, Robert Field, Thomas Carpenter, and Ralph Mackerell.

Several more transfers were made over the next few years, however, before the legal situation was considered entirely satisfactory. Finally, by an indenture dated 16th June, 1617, the Manor of Hungerford was conveyed to Ralph Mackerell (Constable), and 13 other local men 'in trust for the inhabitants'. These 14 men thus became the first feoffees or trustees of the Town and Manor of Hungerford.

The present commoners are those people owning and living in the properties established at the time of the 1612 James I grant. At the time of writing there are 109 properties with common rights in the Town and Manor, (of which three are merely sites of former houses), and a further 19 in the Manor and Liberty of Sanden Fee (of which two are undeveloped). The Town and Manor houses are mostly in the High Street, Bridge Street, and Church Street, and the occasional properties in the centre of the town which do not attract common rights are usually those which were owned by the Dean and Canons of Windsor at the relevant date of 1612.

Davis adds that even the 1617 feoffment did not finally establish the fishing rights. Shortly afterwards, the Crown seems to have repudiated its grant of fishery east of the point where the land boundaries of the manor meet the river; this was in spite of the evidence of the Inquiry of 1611. As a result, since a few years after the feoffment, the fishing has ended at the point just mentioned, known as Bottom Meadow, just east of Denford Bridge at the Manor boundary.

The loss of fishing rights eastward of Hungerford Common must have caused considerable resentment in the town, and in 1634 the Constable of the day, Jehoshaphat Lucas, arranged for a horn to be made, bearing the inscription 'John of Gaunt did give and grant Riall Fishing to Hungerford Towne from Elder Stubbe to Irish Stile excepting some several mill pounds. Jehoshaphat Lucas was Constable in 1634.' The inscription was no doubt intended to reinforce the claim to fishing as in the original grant, but there is no evidence that it was ever so again. The horn, now known as the Lucas Horn, is still used every year at Hocktide to warn the inhabitants of the holding of the Hocktide Court.

Tutti-Day: The Commoner's Penny. Here the Assistant Bailiff who is also Town Crier, is seen in Bridge Street collecting a penny from a commoner who is unable to attend the Hocktide Court. In this photograph of 1914 is Edward Bushnell, who was Town Crier from 1880-1923.

Perhaps at this stage we may digress from the chronological history of the town to enlarge a little on Tutti-Day, which is one of the best known of all ancient English ceremonies still taking place in the late twentieth century.

The chief function of Tutti-Day is the holding of the Hocktide Court, and the other events of the week such as the Ale-Tasting and the Commoners Lunch are largely modern embellishments. The origins of the court in Hungerford are unclear, but probably arose from the ancient 'tourns' which were established over much of the country by the thirteenth century. The following quotation from Sir Arthur Bryant's *The Mediaeval Foundation* (Collins, 1966), describes a tourn:

Twice a year, at Easter and Michaelmas, the sheriff visited every hundred in the shire to hold a tourn or criminal court. Everyone who held freehold land in the hundred except the greater magnates had to attend or be fined for absence. In the tourn or 'law hundred', peasants of villein blood as well as freemen played a part. For by Anglo-Saxon law every layman without land that could be forfeited for felony had to belong to a tithing — a group of neighbours responsible for one another's good conduct. Before the sheriff's annual view of frankpledge as it was called, the bailiff checked the tithing lists of every village in his hundred, crossing out the names of those who had died, and swearing in any lad who had reached the age of twelve, and so become in the eyes of the law a responsible citizen. Then he and every other villager paid his tithing-penny, which constituted, with the various court fees and assized rents, the profits of the hundred jurisdiction.

At the sheriff's tourn every village or township was represented by its reeve and four men who answered for any omission in its public duty and for such offences as ploughing up the king's highway or executing a thief caught red-handed without first securing the official witness of a royal bailiff or coroner. They were responsible too for the townships payment of fines imposed on it for breaches of the regulations for baking of bread and brewing of ale. They had to report to twelve freeholders called the jury of presentment all crimes that had been committed within the township. The tourn dealt also with nuisances like washing clothes in wells and polluting the drinking water. More serious offences were pre-sented by the jury to the royal justices for trial on their next visit to the shire."

The similarities between the Hocktide Court and the ancient tourn are quite striking, and there is little doubt that the ceremonies which still take place today in Hungerford have their origins in these ancient courts of the twelfth and thirteenth centuries.

Summers gives a detailed account of the proceedings and customs of Hocktide as they were enacted at the beginning of the twentieth century, and only minor changes have taken place since, but some detail is perhaps worth noting here.

The proceedings start with the Macaroni Supper held at the John of Gaunt Inn on the Friday of Easter week. The meal of Macaroni cheese and watercress is attended by the Constable and other serving officers of the Hocktide Court, who discuss possible appointments to office at the new court. In bygone days the Macaroni Supper marked the end of the quit rent year, by which time the various town rents and tolls had to be paid to the Constable.

A fairly recent innovation has been the introduction of an evening of Ale-Tasting on the following Monday evening, the night before Tutti-Day itself. All commoners and some invited guests join the Constable and official Ale-Tasters at the Three Swans Hotel to share in the tasting(!) of the ale. A cold buffet is served, and the evening makes a splendid prelude to the important day to come.

The following day, the second Tuesday after Easter, is then the most celebrated day in the Hungerford calendar. Hockney Day, Hock Tuesday, or more usually nowadays Tutti-Day, is when the Hocktide Court, or Commoners Court is held in the Town Hall. Previously it was held at '8 of the clock in the forenoon', but for all of this century it has started at 9 o'clock.

At 8 o'clock, however, the Town Crier, in his role as Bellman and Assistant Bailiff, stands on the balcony of the Town Hall, sounds the Lucas Horn, and summons all commoners to the court with the words: "Oyez! Oyez! All ye Commoners of the Town and Manor of Hungerford are requested to attend your Court House at 9 o'clock this morning on pain of being fined. God Save The Queen!" He then walks the length of the High Street and Bridge Street repeating his call. Summers tells us that at the turn of the century it was customary for the Assistant Bailiff to be supplied at Hocktide with a new official dress, including a grey coat with scarlet facings, and brass buttons, and with a tall hat with gold bands. The dress is the same today, but our present Crier and Assistant Bailiff, Robin Tubb, who has just celebrated 25 years of town crying, has to manage as best he can without the luxury of new dress clothes annually!

A further custom in the early 1900's was that those commoners who were unable to attend court came out into the street and paid the Assistant Bailiff the 'Commoners Penny', which seems to have taken the place of the shilling fine previously. This 'Commoners Penny' is quite separate from the 'head penny' which is collected later in the day by the Tutti-men.

At 9 o'clock prompt, the court convenes in the Town Hall, whilst the two Tutti-men start out on their journey around the old town, accompanied by the Orange-man, a sort of mentor and guide, whose experience over many years is of considerable value to the Tutti-men during their strenuous day.

At the head of the meeting is the Constable, who takes his seat in a carved ebony chair often referred to as the 'John of Gaunt' chair, although it is probably of Portugese origin, and dating from the Elizabethan period! The Lucas Horn is laid before him, and proceedings commence.

The Hocktide Jury of at least 12 commoners is sworn in, and they select a foreman. The roll of commoners is called, and the fines are now paid by a friend so that his right of pasture and fishing is not lost for the following year. The Steward of the Manor then reads the 'Ancient Customs', handed down for generations.

The Common Rights are usually for two or four cows (and maybe one horse also), depending originally on the number of animals the owner could support through the winter months. The rights to fish in the Town and Manor water and to shoot on the Common and Freeman's Marsh, are not transferable, being held by the Commoner in person, who, besides being the owner of the property with rights, must actually live within 5 miles of the Town Hall. It is customary in the present day for the grazing rights to be waived, however, and the Trustees let the grazing to various local farmers. The sum thus raised is used to maintain the common pasture (fence repairs, tree-felling, planting, and fertilizing), and any balance accrues to the general Town and Manor funds for maintaining the Town Hall. Two local farmers (the Harvey brothers) act as Haywards, and have given invaluable service for many years.

Following the reading of the list of Commoners, the Constable next submits the accounts, an item which in previous years must have occupied some considerable time. Quit-rents and tolls are no longer collected, of course, but the fishery accounts, and those of the Town Hall, Common, and John of Gaunt Inn are read and approved before being submitted to the Charity Commissioners.

Then follows the Election of Officers, starting with the Constable. For this, the highest office in the Town and Manor, a candidate must have already served as Tutti-man, Bailiff, and Port-Reeve. Often he is re-elected for a second or third year of office. It is interesting that until 1926 the Constable was also the official Coroner for the area. The Port-Reeve (or Portrieve), whose duty in earlier years was to collect quit-rents, is next elected, but traditionally this position now goes to the Bailiff of the preceeding year.

The Bailiff used to collect the tolls due at the fairs and markets in the town, and as a symbol of authority he has a black, silver mounted staff, bearing the date 1688. Next to be elected are the Water-Bailiffs, now eight in number, reflecting the increasing importance and complexity of caring for the towns stretch of river, and the eight Overseers of the Common (Port Down), whose job is all the more responsible now that the Common is used not only for grazing, but for innumerable sports and activities.

There are three Keepers of the Keys of the Common Coffer, although the Constable is a fourth Keeper during his term of office. Two Ale-Tasters are elected, and four Tutti-men, two of whom retire each year. The office of Bellman and Assistant Bailiff completes the Office Holders – a total of 29 people in 1982. Although some offices (notably those relating to the Fishery and Common) have grown in number in recent years, there are some positions that have fallen from usage. There no longer are two Searchers and Sealers of Leather, or two Tasters of Flesh and Fish!

When the election of officers is completed, various notices and present-ments regarding the administration of the fishery, the Town Hall, and the Common are read, and discussion of these and other matters takes place. When all grievances are aired, and each has had his say, the Commoners Court is closed.

Meanwhile, the Tutti-men have set out on their journey which will last them all day. They carry the famous Tutti-Poles, which are two-metre tall staves, decorated beautifully in a traditional way with spring flowers and ribbons. For many years this has been carried out lovingly by Mrs Jean Tubb, mother of the Town Crier. It is probably these decorated poles that give Tutti-day its name, tutti being a West Country name for a nose-gay, or bunch of sweet-smelling flowers. No doubt the Tutti-men were glad of their tutti's when visiting some of the less sweet-smelling parts of the town in Mediaeval times!

In the past the Tutti-men collected the 'head-penny' from each and every householder (with commoners rights), but this custom lapsed many years ago. Nevertheless, every commoners house is visited during the day, and inevitably the visitors are offered hospitality at each one. Traditionally they were able to ask for a kiss from the lady of the house in addition to the head-penny. This custom has not lapsed(!), and the Tutti-men have been known to use many devices including ladders to achieve their aim! The Orange-man supplies an orange for presentation to each lady kissed. It was mentioned earlier that there are about 100 commoners houses to visit, and it is no wonder that the Tutti-men sometimes look rather the worse for wear. However, the Orange-man, a post filled for many years by Mr 'Bob' Lewington, ensures that all goes well and that the whole hazardous course is completed by the end of the day!

At mid-day there is a luncheon held for all commoners and their invited guests in the Corn Exchange. It was held in the Three Swans Hotel until 1974, but the move to a bigger room has meant that many more Hungerford residents are now able to enjoy the event. During the meal the Ale-Tasters are called upon to judge the quality of the ale being served, using for the purpose the large pewter tankards which are the symbol of their office. Also served at the lunch is 'ye ancient Plantaganet punch' whose recipe was traditionally handed down to successive landlords of the Three Swans.

After the meal, and the speeches by the Constable and his guest speaker, all newcomers to the Tutti-lunch, who are called 'colts', are shod, by having shoeing nails driven into their shoes (and occasionally, it is whispered, their feet!), by the local blacksmith, a post held enthusiastically for many years by Mr Paul Good. The hammering only stops when the colt shouts 'punch' and pays a contribution to his meal. Copper coins, which at one time were heated first, were thrown to the children of the town in the past, but since the move to the Corn Exchange the danger of traffic has prevented this custom whose origin is quite unknown, from continuing. Recently, some coppers are thrown by the Tutti-men during their trip around the town.

The final event of the week is the Hocktide Ball, held recently in the John of Gaunt School, although previously a banquet was held in the Corn Exchange to round off the proceedings. On the following Sunday, the second after Easter, the newly elected Constable leads his office-holders and other town officials and representatives of various organizations to St. Lawrences Church for the 'Constables Service', the Bailiff's staff being carried by the Bellman as they walk in procession.

The customs are carried out today, very much as they would have been many centuries ago. Hungerford's Commoners Court is now unique in the country, the last remaining court with such administrative jurisdiction over its affairs. Let us hope that the traditions will continue to be carefully re-enacted to inspire future generations with thoughts of centuries of rural English history.

The Seventeenth Century and the Civil War

The seventeenth century proved to be an important one for Hungerford. The feoffment of 1617 gave the local people considerable control over their affairs, and the town appears to have prospered. Many of the houses standing in the central part of the High Street (and several in other parts of the town) date from the latter part of the century, although many have been modified since by the addition of new facades. Records show that there were two fairs, and three annual markets, for cattle, for sheep, and wool, and contemporary deeds often mention the associated occupations of tanners, saddlers, fellmongers (dealing with fleeces and hides), mercers, dyers and weavers.

In 1607 a new town hall was built. The first town hall had been mentioned in a survey by the Duchy of Lancaster in 1543/4, in which the 'Courte House' is referred to as being 'ruinous and utterly dekeyed'. Although the age of this first building is not known, an important structure like this may have lasted about 200 years, and if so it was probably erected during the middle of the fourteenth century, perhaps under the instruction of John of Gaunt. This old 'Courte House' stood in the Market Place outside the building now known as The Antiques Arcade.

During the 'Charters Case' in 1573, mention was again made of the 'weakness of the building', and in 1598 is was said to have been 'but meanly repaired'. During the early years of the seventeenth century it had to be replaced, however, for in 1607 'the townsmen of Hungerford have at their own costs and charges builded and erected one house called the Town Hall, wherein the King's Majesty's Courts and Law-Days for the said manor are usually kept, together with a shop under the same Hall, and also two prisons thereunto adjoining for the punishment of malefactors. There is also near adjoining unto the said Town Hall one market house for corn, with a loft over the same, from which there is paid yearly quit-rent to the King 2d.; and not far distant from the same there hath been builded the market house for butter, cheese and other commodities.'

Around the Town Hall stood the usual pillory, stocks and whipping-post. A ducking-stool was kept there, and when required it was wheeled up the High Street for use in the town pond which used to be on the east side of the

High Street opposite the old National School building. Incidentally, the pond is later described as having rails around it, and some lime trees were planted in 1718, but as they failed to thrive they were replaced by firs. The pond was eventually filled up in 1805.

The north gable of the Town Hall contained a 'Clock House', and in 1687 a new clock was bought for £10, a large sum indeed at that time. The clockwinder at the time was John Tubb, and one wonders if the present winder of the clock, Robin Tubb, is a descendant. This Jacobean Town Hall was to last until the latter part of the eighteenth century, when in its turn it too was replaced by a new building.

There are numerous entries in the Hocktide Court records and Constables accounts with regard to the 'town bulls'. The provision of bulls for breeding purposes was usually one of the duties of the lord of the manor, or,

The Town Hall in 1769: This reproduction of a 200 year old print shows the 1607 Town Hall which stood in the Market Place, a little to the south of its 1786 successor (see page 44). The style of the triple gabled building on the right shows a striking resemblance to the present day Antiques Arcade, which dates from the 17th century.

in some places, the local rector. In Hungerford, however, one or sometimes two bulls were bought with town funds, and kept in enclosures on the Port Down, or sometimes by local farmers with whom arrangements had been made to 'summer' or 'winter' them. One extraordinary entry refers to 'backsiding the bull' – which means keeping it in a yard!

The town also owned some swans, and it was customary for the Constable to go on Lammas Day, 1st August, and meet the men who were to mark or 'up' the cygnets hatched during the past year. In 1669 the Constable, Thomas Oram, records that Bulstrode Whitelock's swan marker had forestalled him and had marked them all before he had arrived on the scene!

At one time the town also kept 'stocks' or hives of bees, and some of these were sold in 1674. At a much earlier period, in 1487, 'honey and wax proceeding from the swarms of bees in the Park' are mentioned as Crown property. Other entries in seventeenth century records include 'wanting the downe' (i.e. killing moles on the common) at a price of 2d per skin, clearing the Common of 'yellow-weed' (? rag-wort), and there are further payments for killing other pests such as foxes, weasles, and 'grays' (or badgers).

The event which dominated England in the seventeenth century was the Civil War of 1642-46. Much of the country was affected in one way or another. In the autumn of 1643, the Earl of Essex with the Parliamentary troops relieved Gloucester, and he planned to travel along the Roman Road through Cirencester and Newbury back to London. However, Prince Rupert and the Royalists intercepted Essex on 18th September in the Aldbourne Chase, and a considerable skirmish took place. The result was not decisive, however, and to avoid further hindrance, Essex determined to push on eastwards. He abandoned the planned route along Ermine Street, and marched through Aldbourne itself, where two of his ammunition wagons broke down, reaching Chilton that night. He stayed at the house of Mr John Packer, whilst many of his troops spent the night in Hungerford. Several of the soldiers wounded at Aldbourne Chase were brought to Hungerford and some died here; four were buried on 18th September, and others on the 25th September, and 4th October.

After re-assembling in Hungerford the next morning, and obtaining what refreshment they could, the Parliamentary forces marched on through Kintbury and Hamstead Marshall to Enbourne, intending to spend the night in Newbury. However, Essex found the town was already occupied by Royalist forces, and this led to the 1st Battle of Newbury on Wash Common. Many splendid accounts of both this and the later 2nd Battle of Newbury are available for those who wish to read more on the subject.

Nothing more is heard of either army in the neighbourhood of Hungerford until June 1644, when Essex and his army spent the night of the 10th in the town, whilst on his way to the West Country. On 5th October, the Earl of Manchester, who was then at Reading, reported that most of his horse were at Hungerford, where they stayed until being sent to Salisbury on the 9th.

After the 2nd Battle of Newbury on 27th October 1644, King Charles I assembled the Royalist army in Hungerford, where he was staying at the Bear Inn. On the 19th November he left with his troops, marching north to Shefford en route for Faringdon.

Little more is known of the war around Hungerford, but in 1651, the young King Charles II, having been crowned at Scone, made an attempt to recover his father's kingdom. He was defeated by Cromwell at Worcester on 3rd September, and on the following day the Council of State sent orders to the Militia Commissioners of Hampshire to march their levies (enrolled men), which were then at Hungerford, to join Cromwell at Worcester.

Cromwell was now firmly established as Protector, but not all Royalist opposition was quelled, for, on 11th March 1655, a group of gentry from the west of England entered Salisbury with about 200 horse. The assizes were being held at the time, and the revolutionaries seized the sherriff and judges and held them prisoner whilst they proclaimed the king. They received little support from the neighbourhood, however, and were shortly afterwards captured by a troop of the Parliamentary horse, when several of them were executed and the remainder sold as slaves in Barbados. One of the leading burgesses of Hungerford joined the rising, namely John Lucas, brother of Jehoshaphat who had given the horn to Hungerford in 1634, and perhaps the son of John Lucas, one of the first feoffees. He was taken and beheaded at Salisbury.

So much for the Civil War period. On 4th July 1654, the great diarist John Evelyn visited Hungerford on his return to London from Bath. He stayed at the Bear Inn, and his only recorded comment on the occasion was 'a towne famous for its troutes'!

The year 1665 was notorious for the epidemic of plague which ravaged the country. Smaller outbreaks were frequent throughout the century, Hungerford having suffered badly, for example, in 1603/4, very largely because of the poor sanitary arrangements of the time, with a common ditch or gutter running along the streets in front of the houses serving all drainage purposes. There is some suggestion that the widespread occurence of plague was the reason for the development of the many 'Newtowns' in this area, including, of course, Hungerford Newtown. Perhaps some residents decided to move away from the main towns in the hope of avoiding future' outbreaks. The first time Hungerford Newtown appears by name is on Rocques map of 1761, which would certainly fit this explanation.

Despite the plague, Charles II continued to travel his kingdom – perhaps he actually felt safer away from London, which was the most severely affected area of all. On 26th September he passed through Hungerford, four men having been instructed by the Constable 'to digg ye high waies' in preparation for the King's arrival, each man being paid 3d for his services.

In 1668, the other famous seventeenth-century diarist and Secretary to the Admiralty, Samuel Pepys, visited the town, and dined at the Bear Inn on 10th June, whilst on a journey from Abingdon to Salisbury. He writes: 'So come to Hungerford, where very good troutes, eels, and cray-fish. Dinner; a mean town. At dinner there 12s.'. He took a guide to show him the way to Salisbury, at least until the Cathedral spire was in sight. As we shall see in the next chapter, the roads of the day were still in a dreadful condition, and when Pepys visited Newbury in the same month, June 1668, he lost his way to Reading!

In 1677 Queen Catherine rode through the town on her way to Bath, and in 1687 Mary of Modena, the consort of James II, passed through both on her way to and from Bath. The Princess of Denmark also went there in 1688, and as she came to Hungerford each time the bells were rung, as they have been on all royal visits since the Restoration.

The great frost of 1683-84 must have caused considerable suffering in this small town. It began in early December, producing, it is said, ice up to 18 inches (45cms) thick. Many deer parks were destroyed that winter, and even forest trees such as oak were split by the extreme conditions. The Kennet froze and when the thaw did come, there was inevitably widespread flooding to add to the discomfort.

Soon after this, a very important part of English history took place in Hungerford. The Catholic King James II ascended the throne in 1685, but his reign was not to last long. He became increasingly unpopular and by 1688 there were moves afoot to remove him from the throne. In November that year, the Protestant Prince William of Orange, who had married James' own daughter Mary, landed at the head of a strong army at Brixham, Devon, hoping to obtain considerable support for his cause from the West Country landowners. He then headed for London to claim the throne of England, and on 6th December he left Salisbury, and stayed the night at Colingbourne. The next day he came to Hungerford, and it was here, at the Bear Inn, that he met the Commissioners appointed by James II. A very full account is given by Lord Macaulay:

Late on Thursday, 6th December 1688, the Prince of Orange reached Hungerford. The little town was soon crowded with men of rank and note who came thither from opposite quarters. The Prince was escorted by a strong body of troops. The northern lords brought with them hundreds of irregular cavalry, whose accoutrements and horsemanship moved the mirth of men accustomed to the splendid aspect and exact movements of regular armies.

On the morning of Saturday 8th December, the King's Comissioners, consisting of Lord Halifax, Lord Nottingham, and Lord Godolphin,

The Prince of Orange, who later became King William III.

reached Hungerford. The Prince's bodyguard was drawn up to receive them with military respect. Bentinck welcomed them and proposed to conduct them immediately to his master. They expressed a hope that the Prince would favour them with a private audience; but they were informed that he had resolved to hear them and give an answer in public.

They were ushered into his bedchamber, where they found him surrounded by a crowd of noblemen and gentlemen.

Halifax, whose rank, age, and abilities entitled him to precedence, was spokesman. The proposition which the Commissioners had been instructed to take, was that the points in dispute be referred to Parliament, for which the writs were already sealing; and that in the meantime the Prince's army would not come within 30-40 miles of London. Halifax, having explained that this was the basis on which he and his colleagues were prepared to treat, put into William's hand a letter from the King and retired. William opened the letter and seemed unusually moved. He requested that Lords and Gentlemen, whom he had convoked on this occasion, to consult together, unrestrained by his presence, as to the answer which ought to be returned. To himself he reserved the power of deciding in the last resort after hearing their opinion. He then left them and retired to Littlecote Hall, a manor house situated about two miles off.

That afternoon, the Noblemen and Gentlemen whose advice William had asked, met in the great room of the principal Inn at Hungerford. Oxford was placed in the chair, and the King's overtures were taken into consideration. After much altercation the question was put. The majority was for rejecting the proposition which the Royal Commissioners had been instructed to make. The resolution of the assembly was reported to the Prince at Littlecote. He, however, over-ruled the opinion of his too-eager followers, and declared his determination to treat on the basis proposed by the King. Many of the Lords and Gentlemen assembled at Hungerford remonstrated; a whole day was spent in bickering; but William's purpose was immovable. On his side he made some demands which were put in writing and delivered to Halifax.

On Sunday, 9th December, the Commissioners dined at Littlecote. A splendid assemblage had been invited to meet them. The old hall, hung with coats of mail which had seen the Wars of the Roses, and with portraits of gallants who had adorned the Court of Philip and Mary, was now crowded with Peers and Generals.

After a few days the Prince of Orange left Littlecote, and went on his way to Windsor. During 1689 he was crowned, and later that year he passed through Hungerford again, this time as King William III. No doubt it was a very important day for the town, in view of the role it had played a year previously.

So Hungerford reaches the end of the seventeenth century, and a very eventful one it was. The towns importance had grown largely with the popularity of Bath, and this link was to develop more over the following century as we shall see.

Coaching and the Eighteenth Century

We have seen in the previous chapter that Hungerford was already developing into quite an important small market town by the end of the seventeenth century. Over the next 150 years, however, its prosperity increased even more, as a direct result of its good fortune in lying on one of the most important routes in the country at the time – the London to Bath road. Coaching became a big industry, and Hungerford became a 'coaching town'.

In mediaeval times most tracks served merely to link villages to their local market towns. Near Hungerford, however, there was a more important road from a very early date; a survey of Savernake Forest dated 1228 mentions 'the King's Street, leading from the house of the lepers at Hungerford towards Marlborough'. This Kings Way corresponds roughly with the modern A4 through the forest.

By 1275 there was a bridge over the Kennet – the 'pons de Hungreford' was presumably for the benefit of travellers on the Kings Way. At this early time the road to Newbury probably ran nearer to the river than the present road, linking the hamlets of Denford, Avington, Wawcott and Benham, whilst the 'old and great market road from Hungerford to Newbury' ran on the south bank of the Kennet through Kintbury.

It was during the Elizabethan period that road travel began to be used more widely, for private as opposed to military purposes. The Queen herself visited most of her realm by coach, and one of her coachmen is recorded as dying in Hungerford in 1601. The quality of the roads was terrible, however – rutted and dusty in summer, a mud-bath in winter. Even in 1668 Samuel Pepys lost his way on a journey from Newbury to Reading, and there was a great need for good quality maps. John Ogilby made a vast number of road maps in the 1670's, and his edition of the London to Bath road in 1675 shows two alternative routes near Hungerford. The first left the route taken by the present-day A4 just west of the Kintbury turning, and followed the road along Radley Bottom, Upper Denford, Gipsy Lane, and Leverton to Chilton Foliat, Ramsbury and Marlborough. The second route continued through Charnham Street to Froxfield, through Savernake Forest to Marlborough.

During the early 1700's there was an ever increasing need for road improvement, and various obstacles hindered one's passage locally. In Hungerford a gate and rails were erected in 1733 at the southern limit of the town, presumably in an attempt to keep stray animals from roaming the streets. It is unclear how long this gate stood, although it is clearly marked on the map dating from about 1750, and may have remained in use until the early 1800's.

By 1740 road traffic was increasing further, and there were complaints of poor access to the town via the ford through the River Dun. This ford requires a little explanation. The island on which the War Memorial and Bridge Street now stand had been the site of the old Hospital Priory of St John. This ancient priory was first mentioned in 1232, and was eventually to be dissolved by Henry VIII, although buildings remained on 'the island' until the 1740's. The main access to the town was along a route running diagonally from Charnham Street in front of Riverside to the John of Gaunt Inn, crossing the River Dun by means of a ford through the southern arm of the river. In 1740 a note in the accounts mentions '£27.3s.3d for building a cart bridge next to Charnham Street', and at the same time land was bought from the Bear Inn so that the new Bridge Street might be built in a more direct route across the Priory island, in its present position.

The Eddington Turnpike: Although the London to Bath road through Hungerford was one of the busiest in the country, the north-south road was also a busy turnpike. The closest gate to Hungerford stood at the bottom of Wantage Hill, at the junction of the road to Leverton and Hayward.

In 1744 an Act for repairing the turnpike road from Newbury to Marlborough was passed, and in 1746 the road through Froxfield and Savernake to Marlborough was upgraded to a turnpike.

John Rocque's map of Berkshire 1761 gives considerable detail of the Hungerford area. The Bath Road in Eddington no longer ran through Oxford Street and the village itself, but the new road nearer the river was in use in the present position by Norman's Garage. However, the Salisbury Road was still a mere track, the main route to the south clearly being along the present-day Priory Place, and Priory Road to Sanham Green, and thence along the 'back road' to join what is now the Salisbury Road just south of Hornhill. It was probably at about this time the more direct route up the hill towards Beacon Farm became increasingly used.

In 1752 an enterprising Newbury firm, John Clark & Co., started a Flying Coach service to Bath. It proposed travelling at 4–5 mph, and undertook to perform the whole journey in 12 hours. In the same year, the London to Bath Post Coach took two days for its journey, the average coach weighing over a ton. By 1782 things were only a little better – the London to Bath trip now took 38 hours, and a letter posted on Monday would not be delivered until late on Wednesday, and the reply could not be received until Saturday at the earliest.

Besides the many other hazards of travelling in the late eighteenth century, daylight robberies had become so frequent that the Post Office was driven to the humiliating resort of officially advising the public to cut bank notes in half before sending them in the post, and awaiting confirmation of their safe arrival before dispatching the second half!

The flying coaches were the forerunners of the new mail coaches. The first of these ran in 1784, and perhaps this date more than any other signifies the start of the great 'coaching era'. Hungerford was beginning to bustle now as trade increased in leaps and bounds. Many of the High Street properties were 'modernized' by the addition of new facades, and a new Town Hall was built in 1786 in the Market Place, just north of the older 1607 building. A further boost to trade came with the opening of the Western Canal to Hungerford in 1798, but this is discussed in the next chapter.

The hey-day of coaching was to last nearly 60 years, and there is no doubt that these 60 years were some of Hungerford's best. Perhaps the greatest years of all were 1830–40, and dictionaries and almanacs abound with information on coaches and coaching inns. The following detailed information relates to the year 1836.

Of the many large and well-known companies, there were five who operated the Bath Road through Hungerford. There was enormous competition between them, each company priding itself, and advertising its claim, in offering greater comfort, greater punctuality, or above all, greater speed. The race was on – a journey from London to Bath was 108 miles, and to Bristol was 123 miles, and this was a very considerable test of anyone's stamina! At best it took about 13 hours, and at night nearer 18 hours.

The coaches were all named, and these names conjure up a little of the sense of adventure that accompanied travelling in those days: The Emerald, The Age, and The Monarch. Some took their names from their destination – The White Hart, and The York House, whilst another was called the Regulator, presumably promising to run especially punctually! More were utilitarian in their title, maybe resting on their companies good name for advertisement – The General Stage Company's Night (or Day) Coach, or Cooper's Company Night (or Day) Coach.

All the ten mentioned above travelled the Bath Road every day through Hungerford, usually starting at 6–7 a.m. and arriving at their destination by the early evening, whilst the night coaches left at 3.30-5 p.m. and arrived the next morning. A local 'Coach and Carriers Guide' states that there were 200 coaches per week on the Bath Road.

The most spectacular of all, however, were the Royal Mail Coaches, which were operated on this route by W. Chaplin & Co. They managed the journey to Bath in 11½ hours, and to Bristol in 12¼ hours. These were overnight trips, taking mail from one town in the evening for delivery in the other next morning, and their speed is quite remarkable when compared with the usual night trip of 18 hours.

There were, of course, many other services besides these long distance ones. London to Marlborough, Reading to Bath, several on the Oxford to Salisbury route, all ran through Hungerford, in addition to many local ones, such as Palmer's single return journey from Hungerford to Newbury on Tuesday, Thursday, and Saturday each week.

Hungerford is just about halfway between London and Bath; indeed, Halfway hamlet is said to have derived its name thereby. Both Speenhamland and Marlborough were certainly more important as stopping places, but changes of horses were often made every 8–10 miles, and Hungerford must have been quite busy enough, as is confirmed by the large number of inns along Charnham Street and High Street.

Pigots Directory of 1840 names 12 coaches making 35 runs weekly from the following eight inns: The Bear, The Three Swans, The Red Lion, The Stag's Head, The Lamb, The Sun, and The Craven Arms. Old Moore's Almanac of 1836 also mentions The Stag (not Stag's Head), The Swan, The Green Dragon, The White Bear, The Three Horseshoes, and The Queen and Constitution. Others can be found in other directories, and on the 1819 Enclosure Award Map.

The most famous of all Hungerford's inns is The Bear. It may have originated as early as 1297, but there is a definite record in 1494, and many references from 1537 onwards. In 1537 the landlord Robert Brayborn is

The Bear Corner, c. 1908: For centuries the Bear has served travellers on the Bath Road, but the approach road to the town itself was only made in the 1740's, before which access was through a ford, alongside the island on which St John's Priory used to stand.

recorded as giving evidence against three highwaymen who had stopped at the inn, and who were accused of robbing a merchant between Bagshot and Windsor. During the reign of Henry VIII The Bear, along with the manor of Chilton Foliat of which it was part, was settled on five of his six wives, Ann Boleyn being the exception. Shortly after, in 1545 the manor of Chilton Foliat passed to the Darrell family, and in 1607 to Sir John Popham. It is the arms of the Leybourne–Pophams which are incorporated in the handsome sign over the main door in Charnham Street. Its name probably derives from 'The Bear and Ragged Staff', which was the badge of the Earls of Warwick, who were owners of the estate in earlier days.

The 1796 edition of Pigot's Directory calls The Black Bear a 'well accustomed inn', and mentions that 'gentlemen of the neighbourhood have a monthly subscription club and assembly there. The Black Bear finally dropped its 'Black' at the end of the nineteenth century.

There were many other inns along Charnham Street. The Crown (now Undy's Farm) stood at the corner of the Bath Road with the Chilton Foliat road. This corner is referred to as Crown Corner on the 1819 map. The Sun survives to the present day, but further along were The Swan, possibly the present day newsagents and confectioners, and The Stag (or Stag's Head). Charnham Close was The Green Dragon (as well as having been the workhouse at a slightly later period before the new building in Park Street was built). The White Hart was built in about 1686 on the site of the present day café and squash club ground. In 1868 it was sold with the surrounding land for the purpose of building the Wesleyan Chapel, which was erected in 1870. Next door was The Red Lion, and opposite was The Lamb, both of which are still trading, as well as The White Bear in Faulkner Square.

In Eddington was The Three Horseshoes, which was demolished in the nineteenth century to make way for the Eddington Engineering Works, now Christmas Crafts. It is possible that the 'Horseshoe Cottage' opposite derives its name from connection with the inn. Further along Oxford Street near Linden Cottage was The Queen and Constitution, presumably renamed during the nineteenth century.

Back in the main town of Hungerford is the John of Gaunt Inn in Bridge Street, which is owned by the Town and Manor Charity. It dates from the early nineteenth century, and was probably the old workhouse before this. Further up the High Street stands The Three Swans, and standing as it does in the very heart of the old town overlooking the market place, it must have been a very popular hostelry. In addition to these, many other inns have come and gone at various periods in the history of the town.

The coaching hey-day of the 1830's gave way to a complete collapse in the 1840's and 1850's. The early success of the Rocket in 1830 soon led to a rapidly increasing network of railways over the next decade or two. Brunel's Western Railway through Swindon opened in 1841 and as early as 1842 Pigot's Directory shows only two services on the Bath road, but it does advertise conveyance on the railway, the nearest station to Hungerford being Faringdon Road, 14 miles away! There was no regular transport to that station, however, although there were fairly regular coaches to the station at Reading.

It was not long before Hungerford itself was served by the railway. In 1847 a line from Newbury extended the Berkshire and Hampshire Railway to a terminus station at Hungerford, about which more is written in the next chapter. Suffice to say that it sapped the town's prosperity in many ways, and as far as coaching was concerned the bubble had burst. In 1847 the same two services ran as in 1842, but by 1869 the local directories advertised 'Fly's from The Bear and The Three Swans to meet every train', with no mention now of any coach service.

So the end of an era. The popularity of Bath had brought great prosperity to Hungerford, but no doubt the working men and women had worked hard for any gain. It was going to prove equally tough to adjust to the end of the era, but Hungerford was more fortunate than some country towns, as we shall see in the next chapter.

The Canal, The Railway and The Victorian Era

The Kennet and Avon Canal runs through the very heart of Hungerford, and whilst in the present day it provides a source of recreation and enjoyment for all ages, in early times it played a big part in the town's economic development.

As early as 1708 a Bill to make the River Kennet navigable from Reading to Newbury was introduced into Parliament, firmly supported by Hungerford and several Wiltshire towns which would benefit from cheaper rates of goods transport. There was considerable opposition from Reading, whose tradesmen feared loss of custom when people no longer had to travel to their town to buy and sell. Despite these protests, however, the Kennet Navigation Bill received Royal Assent in September 1715, and the navigation was eventually fully open to traffic in 1723.

In 1770 the management began to study the possibility of linking the river Kennet to the River Avon by means of a new canal. The original planned route was by way of Hungerford, Marlborough, Calne, and Chippenham to Bath. Nothing came of this idea at first, and, on 10th March, 1788, a meeting took place in Hungerford to promote the scheme. A second meeting, chaired by Charles Dundas, JP of Barton Court, Kintbury, followed on 16th April.

At both meetings there was general approval of the scheme, and further meetings were held throughout the year to get the support of local land-owners and other interested parties. A pamphlet was published, showing the advantages of the proposed canal: 'The price of carriage of coals, and other heavy articles, will be greatly reduced; the estates of gentlemen and farmers will be improved at much easier expense by the introduction of free-stone, timber, brick, tile, and other building materials; lime, peat-ashes and manure of all sorts. They will find new markets for the produce of their farms and estates; corn, malt, cheese, and other productions, will meet with a ready and cheap conveyance to the great marts.'

Three engineers were consulted, and they reported the results of their surveys in the summer of 1789. Each favoured the route via Hungerford, Ramsbury and Marlborough to Bath, but even at this stage there was a little anxiety about the adequacy of the water supply to the summit, although further engineers felt it would be satisfactory.

The Western Canal committee asked John Rennie to make a detailed survey of the route, and after he too had declared the water supply was satisfactory, a meeting was held at Marlborough in November 1790, when it was decided to go ahead with the proposed junction canal at an estimated cost of £213,940.

However, the original subscription target of £75,000 was not met, only £17,700 being received, and it was not until 1792 that the money was found to revive the Western Canal. Around this time it actually became quite easy to fund any new canal – during this time of 'canal mania' an enormous number of canals were projected, and an even greater number of sponsors were eager to jump on the band wagon! Soon a sum of no less than £1,000,000 was pledged for the Western Canal.

In July 1793, Rennie reported the results of his latest survey: he had changed his mind about the route, now favouring a more southerly route via Great Bedwyn, Devizes and Trowbridge. Marlborough would still be served, but by a branch canal from Hungerford. A tunnel 4,312 yards long would be required at the new summit level, but he stated that this new route would be cheaper, and would be completed more quickly than the original one. His revised plan was approved at a meeting at the Castle Inn, Marlborough in August 1793, Rennie taking the opportunity to explain his increasing anxiety about the adequacy of water to the summit of the old route. It was at a meeting in September in the same year that the name of the project was changed to the Kennet and Avon Canal.

The year 1793 had seen the outbreak of the French Revolution, and with it a financial crisis in England. Rising costs were the inevitable result, and the estimated cost of the Kennet and Avon had risen to over £375,000 excluding the Marlborough branch. The committee agreed in January 1794 to abandon plans for the branch, agreeing instead to a rebate of 2d per ton on all goods carried on the Kennet and Avon Canal that were destined for Marlborough.

In April, 1794, the Bill for cutting the canal received Royal Assent, and John Rennie was appointed engineer in May. A further survey, this time by William Jessop, recommended altering the line of the canal to avoid the $2\frac{1}{2}$ mile tunnel. Additional locks would be required at Crofton, together with a steam engine to raise water to the new summit level, but there would nevertheless be a considerable saving in terms of construction time and cost, the new tunnel at the summit level being only 500 yards long.

Work started both at Newbury and Bradford-on-Avon in October 1794, and proceeded steadily. However, the inflationary effect of the Napoleonic Wars resulted in a quarter of the shareholders being behind with their payments by July 1796, and by April 1797 work on the canal had to be slowed considerably.

However, Walter Money, in his History of Newbury 1887, was able to report that 'the first section of the Kennet and Avon Canal between Newbury and Kintbury, a distance of six milies, was opened on June 12th, 1797. A barge of nearly 60 tons, having on board the band of the 15th Regiment of Dragoons, then stationed in Newbury, left that place at twelve o'clock and arriving at Kintbury at half-past two, where the Committee of the Canal, having dined with the Chairman, Mr Charles Dundas, embarked at six o'clock, and arrived at Newbury about half-past nine, the passage of the party affording great interest to a large number of persons assembled at different points on the route.'

Despite growing financial problems with the company, progress at the eastern end was good: the Kintbury to Hungerford section was opened in October 1798. The Bath Chronicle reported that on 'Tuesday the ninth instant, a Barge, having on board a staircase of wrought Portland Stone for J. Pearce, Esq., of Chilton Lodge, several casks of Russian tallow, . . . making in the whole about 40 tons weight, was navigated on the Kennet and Avon Canal from Newbury to Hungerford.'

THE CANAL, HUNGERFORD

The Canal: The barge is passing the 'winding-hole' or turning area and approaching Hungerford bridge and wharf. Clearly the popularity of canal fishing is nothing new!

Progress continued, and within a few months 'the navigation of the Kennet and Avon Canal was opened from Hungerford to Great Bedwyn on July 2nd, 1799, when a barge of 50 tons, laden with coals and deals, arrived at the latter place. The barge, having on board a large number of inhabitants of Hungerford, was accompanied on its passage by a vast concourse of people, and received at Bedwyn with great demonstrations of joy. An entertainment was provided at the Town Hall, and a quantity of beer distributed to the populace and the labourers employed on the canal. The evening concluded with great festivity.' (Money ibid).

Although progress at both the western and eastern ends of the canal was good, the central portion, from Devizes to Great Bedwyn was not completed for another ten years. The first barge to ascend the Caen Hill flight at Devizes, which was the last part of the canal to be completed, did so on 28th December, 1810, and after 40 hard years, the dream of a through passage connecting Reading and Bath was realized.

At the time of the opening of the canal, Hungerford was enjoying the prosperous years of the coaching period. The building of a new wharf right in the very centre of the town, of which the stone warehouse, now converted into two houses, is the only remaining sign, brought further trade and prosperity to the town.

Two important buildings were erected at this time, and it is interesting to note the utilization of Bath Stone, brought by canal, and previously unused in the town. Firstly the new church: at the beginning of the nineteenth century the Early English-style church, which had stood for about 600 years, had become so delapidated that it was in danger of collapse, and services could not be held in bad weather. In 1811 major repairs and partial rebuilding were undertaken, but no sooner was the work completed than part of the original building collapsed, bringing with it the newly built tower. There was clearly no alternative now but to build a completely new church, and in 1814 an Act of Parliament was obtained, authorizing the Vicar, Church Wardens and Trustees to raise £6,000 for the task. In the end it was actually to cost nearly £30,000, the balance being obtained partly by private donation, and partly by a tontine. Between 1814 and 1816 the remaining portion of the ancient church was demolished, the whole site was cleared, and in its place a new Georgian Gothic building was erected, designed by Mr Pinch of Bath, modelled on his church at Bathwick. It was therefore not surprising that it should be constructed of Bath stone.

1814 also saw the foundation of Hungerford's National School – the Church of England based institution for primary education, at a cost of one penny per week. Previously the only day school in the town was the free Grammar School in The Croft, founded in 1653 by Dr Sheaff, but places here were very limited. The new National School was built towards the southern end of the High Street, on the west side, and although the school building was of brick, the adjacent house was refurbished and clad in Bath stone, for use by the master.

The economic climate of the time brought about the development of banks, and Hungerford saw its first savings bank in 1816, further increasing its importance as a local market centre.

A chart of trade on the Kennet and Avon in 1814 shows the most important cargoes being carried at the time: coal from Wales, Somerset and Gloucestershire was being carried eastwards along the whole length of the canal, as was building stone from Bath. Limestone from Bristol and Bath was carried to Newbury and Reading, as were slates from the port at Bristol. Flints came west from Reading, as did peat ash from Aldermaston. Tin plate, iron, copper, and salt, timber and pitch from the West Indies, and tea from the East Indies, were all carried.

The wharf at Hungerford was especially busy loading gravel, chalk and whiting for the westerly route, and timber for the east. Grain and flour were very plentiful here, and a fairly equal volume went in both directions.

In 1818, over 200 boats were using the canal, some seventy of these were barges of over 60 tons capacity. The average time taken to travel the 57 miles journey from Newbury to Bath was 3 days 9 hours.

It has already been mentioned that many of the High Street properties had had modern frontages added during the latter half of the eighteenth century, but the double effect of the coaching trade and the canal trade brought even greater prosperity during the first four decades of the nineteenth century. The High Street was developed further south up the hill, and new properties were built along Church Street (then Church Lane), Park Street (then Cow Lane), and Charnham Street.

Census figures show an increase in the towns population from 1,987 in the year 1801 to 2,696 by the year 1851, a very considerable growth of 35 per cent. Incidentally, the returns show that despite the importance of trading and marketing, no less than 77 per cent of the adult population of the area was involved in farmwork in the year 1851.

The prosperous years of the Kennet and Avon ended in 1852. Isambard Kingdom Brunel's Great Western Railway Act was passed in 1835, and such was the speed of railway construction that the line from London to Bristol was fully open by June 1841. Local canal traffic continued for several years because the route of the railway was some way to the north, through Swindon, but the long distance trade virtually stopped overnight. The Canal Company was taken over by the GWR in 1852, and thereafter the canal succumbed to the inevitable neglect.

Hungerford might have expected that its problems would be solved if the railway could be brought to the town. Indeed, it was not long before just that happened, for a double track broad gauge line was extended to Hungerford from the Newbury 'Berkshire and Hampshire Railway', and the first station, a terminus building, was opened on 21st December, 1847.

In 1859, a local company proposed the building of what became the 'Berkshire and Hampshire Extension Railway', a 24 mile extension of single track onward from Hungerford westwards to Seend near Devizes, where it was to link with a branch of the Wilts, Somerset and Weymouth Railway. The line was opened in November 1862, and its construction had a considerable effect on the appearance of Hungerford. In the first place, the original terminus station was altered to allow through traffic, and for the first time the broad High Street was spanned by a railway bridge (later replaced in 1898 when the line was converted to double track). A high embankment was built through the very heart of the town, and three more bridges were built, in Croft Lane, Parsonage Lane, and Marsh Lane (all later enlarged to carry the double track). In 1874 the line was changed from broad gauge to the new standard gauge.

G. W. R. Station, Hungerford.

The Station: The buildings on the left are part of the original 1847 terminus station, which was modified in 1862 when the line was extended on through the town. The up-line buildings, and the pedestrian bridge were built at the turn of the century. The old station was demolished in 1964 and only the bridge (without its canopy) and the name-boards now remain.

The expected prosperity as a result of the railway never materialized, however. So many towns now had their own stations that there was little need to travel to Hungerford. What the railway did bring though was the tendency for some of the population to move away from this rural area towards the bigger towns and cities, where work was expected to be more plentiful and better paid. Indeed, the population of Hungerford actually fell from 2,696 in the year 1851 to 2,513 in the year 1901.

The Canal trade was still limping on – during the 1870's and 1880's repeated leaks, and progressive silting up led to increasing delays, but despite these complications several steamboats battled to ply a speedy service. C. Evans & Co. operated 'Spitfire' and 'Express' between Hungerford and Reading.

In 1877, though, the Canal Company made its first deficit, and it was never to make a profit thereafter. The table shows the trade figures in various years for the canal as a whole, and also the tonnage loaded at Hungerford wharf.

YEAR	TOTAL	H'FORD
1812	126,299	
1823	188,704	
1848	360,610	
1858	261,822	
1860	240,547	3,133
1868	210,567	
1880		2,317
1890	163,565	3,646

It is intriguing that the trade at Hungerford wharf held up so well at a time when the overall canal trade was in such decline, and when the population of the town was actually falling.

Despite the problems, however, civic pride ran high, and, in the late 1860's the decision was taken to replace the old and unsafe town hall standing in the market place with a fine new building, incorporating a large Corn Exchange. The foundation stone was laid in September 1870, and it was built in red brick with yellow terracotta decoration, in the Byzantine style peculiar to the later Victorians, on land bought from the church in exchange for other land on the common. The total cost was about £4,000, and the Corn Exchange opened for business in October 1871. The clock tower of the new building was designed to accommodate the old town hall clock, which had been presented to the town a few years earlier by a benefactor.

During the Victorian period there was much new church building in Hungerford. The Congregational Church in the High Street had been built in 1840, the Primitive Methodist Chapel in Bridge Street in 1864, and the

The Old Town Hall: This building, erected in 1786, stood in the Market Place, opposite Cow Lane (now Park Street). By the 1860's, the building was in a poor state of repair, and the much larger new Corn Exchange was built nearby in 1870-71. The town hall clock had been given by a benefactor during the 1860's, and the new Corn Exchange tower was designed to accommodate the old clock.

Wesleyan Chapel in Charnham Street (now demolished) in 1869. The Church of England parishioners now looked to their church of St Lawrence, and sought to make some improvements. The original design by Mr Pinch had been unsatisfactory in many ways, and between 1879 and 1887 very extensive reconstructions and alterations were made, including the rebuilding of the clerestory, and the replacement of the painted iron pillars supporting the roof by arcades of Bath stone columns. The present organ was installed in the west gallery at this time.

Although the population had been falling, there was a strong effort made to develop some industrial employment in the town at this time. Two firms in particular are worthy of special mention. Messrs Cottrell & Co. was an engineering firm in the Eddington iron works (now Christmas Crafts and Normans Garage). Their entry in Kelly's Directory describes them as 'iron founders, millwrights, agricultural implement and boiler makers; patentees of the 'Climax' (gold medal) folding elevator and prize medal engines and water carts'. Not to be outdone by their competitors, the other local

The Two Town Halls: For a few months only were there two Town Halls in Hungerford. In the foreground is the 1786 building, its clock tower (built only a few years earlier to accommodate the clock given by a benefactor) is empty, the clock having been transferred to the tower of the new Town Hall behind. Between January and April 1872 the old building was demolished, some of the materials being used to build cottages in Church Street.

engineering firm of Messrs Henry Gibbons, of the Kennet Works (site of Stirlands Service Station now) advertised themselves as 'manufacturer of Gibbons' patent moulding machines, lawn mower sharpeners, patent safety flush bolts and manufacturers of steam and hot water fittings and all kinds of agricultural implements (medals awarded)'. Both firms were known for the high quality of their work, and they must have contributed much to the town's strength during those difficult years towards the end of the nineteenth century.

In 1894 the municipal boundaries were changed, so that Leverton became part of the parish of Hungerford, and Charnham Street, along with North and South Standen, were transferred from Wiltshire to Berkshire. For the first time then, Charnham Street became a true part of the town, and with Eddington, Hungerford approached the twentieth century a much bigger administrative unit.

Oxford Street, Eddington at the turn of the Century: The grocery store on the right was run by two Misses Winkworth, and although now a private house, the 'shop' window and doorway are unchanged today. On the left is a group of workers at the wheelwrights and blacksmith, now demolished along with several buildings on that side of the street. At the far end of this part of Oxford Street is Linden Cottage, where the road turns towards Eddington Bridge.

Charnham Street in 1906: Despite a hot summer's day, there are some fine examples of Edwardian dress – possibly it is literally the 'Sunday best'. The background buildings are largely unchanged today.

The Twentieth Century and the Town Today

Hungerford has grown more in the last 80 years than at any stage in its history, its population having more than doubled over the period. Despite this, it has managed to retain a remarkably unspoiled High Street, and, standing as it does in an area of 'outstanding natural beauty', planning restrictions have now largely contained its spread.

By the early 1900's the administration of the Town and Manor by the Feoffment established in 1617 had survived almost unaltered for nearly 300 years. The setting up of the Charity Commissioners, however, brought every charity in the land under scrutiny, and in 1905 it was the turn of Hungerford to submit reports on all its local charities. These included, of course, not only all the local educational charities, but also the 1617 feoffment. There was extensive correspondence between the feoffees and the Charity Commissioners over several issues, chief of which was whether the various 'rights' should be restricted to 'commoners' only, or extended to all 'inhabitants' of the town. However, it was eventually confirmed that only those occupiers of the original 1612 properties would be able to claim 'commoners rights', although the various Common Lands would continue to be for the benefit of all inhabitants. Eventually, in 1908, the Trustees became responsible to the Charity Commissioners under a scheme registered as the Town and Manor of Hungerford Charity.

Several new town buildings were erected around this time – St John's Mission Hall had been built in 1899, Church House (on the site of the old free Grammar School) in 1900, and the Church House Club, later Hungerford Club, was formed in 1901. In 1903 the Hungerford Water Works company was established, and in 1909 a mains drainage scheme was installed.

The new school in Fairview Road was built in 1910, and with it the various church schools in the town closed. The old National School in the High Street continued to be used for educational purposes, however, until the mid 1960's when it was let for commercial use before being sold in 1973.

The outbreak of war in 1914 had a profound effect on Hungerford. A large number of families sent men to fight, and 76 lost their lives during those terrible four years. But the men and women at home played their part:

Hungerford was soon to find itself very much involved with the war preparations. In January 1915, the newly formed army unit (180 Company, Royal Army Service Corps, Mechanical Transport) arrived in the town, which was to be its mobilization station. Initially the unit was small, comprising one officer and 32 men, with one car, two motor cycles, and 15 lorries! The vehicles were parked in the High Street to start with, whilst The Croft was used as their parade ground.

Over the next few months the unit was gradually expanded, until in July it was complete, and fully prepared for battle. By this time there were nearly 500 men and 109 vehicles, and on 23rd July 1915, the whole company assembled in the High Street, and watched and cheered by the whole town, they set off on their way to Avonmouth, bound for France. Hungerford had certainly done its best over those six months to help the war effort, and the gratitude of the Company is amply recorded in its Historical Record.

During the war both the National School and Church House were taken over for use as hospitals for the treatment of men wounded in the fighting.

As the country struggled to recover after the war, Hungerford sought to build a memorial to those local men who had lost their lives. At the time, the old International Stores in Bridge Street had closed, and it was decided to demolish the building along with the adjacent houses, and to erect a War

Off to The Front: The morning of 23rd July 1915, and the whole of the 180 Company R.A.S.C., M.T. are assembled in the High Street, prior to leaving for France. About 500 men and 109 vehicles were in the parade.

Memorial on the site, between the two arms of the River Dun, taking the opportunity to widen the narrow Bridge Street at the same time. The Memorial and Gardens were dedicated in November 1920, at a service attended by most of the town. It is interesting to note when visiting the Memorial that it stands on the site of the old Priory of St. John, and that the main access to the town before 1740 was via the ford through the adjacent river.

The years after the First World War saw the town begin its great 20th century expansion. At the turn of the century there were few buildings outside the main five roads – High Street, Bridge Street, Charnham Street, and Park Street. Gradually, Fairview Road, The Croft, Prospect Road, and Priory Road were all extended and developed.

This was a time of great community spirit, with a strong emphasis locally on sports and games, which took place on a more or less competitive basis! A golf course had opened on the Common at the beginning of the century; it lapsed for many years before re-opening in 1929. It was still not viable, however, and closed again in 1931. The sports ground in The Croft was opened in 1921, and bowls, croquet, and tennis were very popular. Shooting, football, rugby, and cricket all thrived. In the canal there were several swimming races and water sports held, a starting board being placed across the canal by the town bridge, the course going up towards the town lock and back.

The various water mills in the area had mostly closed by now. The Town Mill (or Queens Mill) in Bridge Street, which had operated since at least 1576, closed after the war and was later demolished and replaced by a private house (Mill Hatch). There was, however, a large corn mill operating in the town: the old nineteenth century brewery standing in Everlands Road (initially Platts Brewery, but later taken over by the South Berks Brewery) had closed, and the building was converted to a mill by the local firm of James, which operated here for many years, before moving in 1931 to a new larger purpose-built mill in Church Street, in what was previously the large garden of Kennet House.

During the Second World War the Kennet and Avon Canal became a line of defence across the south of the country in case of invasion. Numerous 'pillboxes' were built along its length, some of which remain today. In the town there were 'tank traps' under the railway bridge, and a large gun-emplacement outside Pratts butchers shop (now John Lewis kitchens). Large numbers of American troops were stationed in the area, especially on the Chilton and Littlecote estates, and the airfields of Rudge, Membury, and Welford were developed. In 1944 General Eisenhower himself came to Hungerford to speak to a large force of his troops assembled on the Common just prior to D-Day.

Hungerford's memorial to the 28 men whose lives were lost during the

1939-45 war, was the development of a 12 acre Recreation area, on land leased from the Town and Manor. The whole ambitious scheme, including the Avenue of Remembrance (with its 28 trees), Sarsen Stone, childrens recreation area, cricket pitch, and playing fields, was opened in 1949. On an adjacent site, in 1964, the open-air swimming pool was opened, prior to which swimming was allowed in the Bathing Place in the River Kennet. The pool cost about £14,000, partly financed by profits from the town carnivals, which were restarted in 1958.

Another amenity in the town was the cinema. In the early 1900's films had been shown in the Corn Exchange, but in 1934 a cinema was built in Church Way at the top of Atherton Road. Along with so many similar buildings, it became unprofitable in the late 1960's and closed in 1972 before being demolished in 1974 to make way for housing. It is nice that its name is preserved in the road of its site – Regent Close.

The expansion of Hungerford accelerated after the Second World War, with both private and council housing extending its limits considerably. The table below shows the dates of development of some of the newer roads in the town. The dates can only be approximate as there was a span of several years in most cases.

Priory Avenue	1955	Regent Close	1975
Chilton Way	1961	Uplands	1975
Macklin Close	1967	Lancaster Close	1976
Lancaster Square	1967	Bourne Vale	1977
Sanden Close	1967	de Montfort Grove	1977
Homefield Way	1967	York Road	1977
Park Way	1970	Morley Place	1978
Coldharbour Road	1970	Westbrook Close	1980
Clarkes Gardens (end)	1971	Chantry Mead	1980
Orchard Park Close	1973	Chilton Way	1980
Hillside Road	1973	Combe View	1983
Canal Walk	1973		

In 1959 a new doctors surgery was built in The Croft, and the old Manor House in the High Street, which had been used as the surgery until this date, was sold. Sadly, in what must rank as one of the worst planning decisions in Hungerford's development, this fine historic building was demolished in 1965 to make way for a petrol filling station. It did not last long, however, and eventually, in 1975 the site was redeveloped, and International Stores opened a new supermarket. Even now the design of the original Manor House doorway is retained in the centre of the shop front.

Another change in the town's appearance came in June 1960, when James & Co. Great Western Mill in Church Street caught fire during the night, and was burned to the ground. As a result it was decided to rebuild the mill on a new and larger site at the western end of the town at Smitham Bridge. The vacant site was used partly as a car-park, but also for the County Library (opened in 1967) and the new Fire Station (1968).

The original fire-pump had been kept in the Town Hall during the nineteenth century, but when Hungerford's first steam fire engine came in 1891, it was clearly necessary to find a permanent building for it. The town's first fire station was duly built in Charnham Street in 1892, and Hungerford's fine volunteer fire brigade had a permanent home. In 1910 they took possession of a new and more powerful 'Merryweather' steam fire engine, and most of the town came to watch a demonstration of its power on the canal wharf. It is nice to note that it took no less than 20 minutes to get up enough steam pressure to start the engine! In 1924 the local fire service had its first motorised engine, named 'John of Gaunt', and although there have been many successors to this vehicle over the years, the town is very fortunate to have a dedicated and expert fire brigade, still maintained on a voluntary part-time basis.

By the early 1960's, the town had grown to such an extent that the 'council' school in Fairview Road was grossly overcrowded. The local

'The Dreadnought': Hungerford's new Merryweather steam fire-engine came in 1910. The wicker basket was used as a filter over the end of the hose to protect the pump from silt. There was little provision for carrying spare hoses, and the vehicle behind was used to bring extra firemen and hoses to a fire. The picture was taken in Charnham Street, with the Bear Hotel in the background on the left.

Canal Bridge, and Lower High Street c. 1920: Rarely would it be safe nowadays to stand where this boy did! Notice the gas lamps, and the shop on the bridge making and repairing umbrellas.

education authority therefore built a new secondary school for the area (including Lambourn and Kintbury), and the new John of Gaunt School was opened on its spacious site at the south-eastern edge of the town in 1963. The continuing expansion of the town since then has led to the primary school being one of the largest in Berkshire.

Also in the 1960's it became clear to the Trustees that extensive work was required to renovate the Town Hall and Corn Exchange. It has already been stated that Hungerford's Town Hall is the only one in the country not municipally owned and financed from the rates, and it was equally clear to the Trustees that general Town and Manor funds could not finance the work. The Constable of the day, Mr John Newton, himself a steam enthusiast, spearheaded the organization of several Steam Fairs held annually over a summer weekend on the Common. They were very successful, and the restoration of the 100-year-old building was started in 1971.

During the eighteenth century, Hungerford had benefitted greatly by lying on the Bath Road. By the mid-twentieth century, however, this situation was no longer to the town's advantage, and at times traffic in the town was seriously congested as a result of 'jams' at the Bear corner. The opening of the M4 motorway in 1971 brought considerable relief, and Hungerford was able to breathe again.

Although there have been antique shops in Hungerford for a very long time, the 1970's saw a rapid growth of the trade locally, with many new shops and a large 'arcade' opening, and regular antiques fairs being held in the Corn Exchange. With the re-opening of the Kennet and Avon Canal in 1974, and with the increasing importance of Littlecote Park as a major tourist attraction, Hungerford is gradually becoming more involved with tourism, a trend that will no doubt continue through the rest of this century.

The broadening of the town's horizons has especially been apparent, through the successful twinning with the French town of Ligueil. The project was promoted by Mr Jack Williams, one of Hungerford's first mayors, and after many months of negotiations and meetings, the final signing of the twinning treaties took place at Ligueil in 1980, and at Hungerford in February 1981. Already there have been many exchange visits which have been much enjoyed by the residents of both towns.

Hungerford today is a thriving and a caring town, larger now than at any stage in its history; large enough to be virtually self-sufficient, and yet small enough to retain that sense of rural stability and permanence founded on its long and interesting history. The residents are fortunate indeed in having so close to the town, the common, the marsh, and the canal, each offering different opportunities for recreation, and fortunate also in living in a town with such an unspoiled main street. Perhaps this short book will help us all, both residents and visitors alike, to appreciate this historic small town, at the western edge of Royal Berkshire.

Diary of Key Events

1108	First mention of a church at Hungerford.
1170	Burgesses of Hungerford used a 'common seal'.
1200	Probable period of new town layout.
1228	Survey of Savernake Forest mentions leper house at Hungerford.
1232	Priory of St John established on 'Bridge Street' island.
1241	Town call a 'borough' for the first time.
1273	Chantry of Blessed Virgin Mary mentioned.
1275	'Pons de Hungreford' mentioned.
1275	Two water mills in the town.
1296	First mention of a market.
1325	Robert de Hungerford founded Chantry of Holy Trinity.
1334	Hungerford still taxed as a 'rural community'.
1340	John of Gaunt born.
1348-50	The Black Death.
1360's	Probable date of the old 'Courte House'.
1361	Town Fair mentioned.
1362	John of Gaunt's wife Blanche inherits Lancastrian estates.
1366	Earliest mention of Hungerford in Duchy records.
1386	Duchy survey makes no mention of a 'borough'.
1446	'Town' and 'borough' mentioned in grant to Lord Hungerford.
1494	Denne Myll (Dun Mill) mentioned.
1494	The Bell Inn mentioned.
1537	Bear Inn landlord gives evidence against highwaymen.
1541	Bear Inn passed to Henry VIII's wives.
1548	Priory of St John dissolved by Henry VIII.
1568-1611	Long wrangle with Duchy over status of townsmen.
1600's	Two fairs and three markets annually.
1601	Queen Elizabeth's coachman died and buried here.
1607	Second Town Hall built.
1617	Debate with Duchy finally settled by Feoffment.
1643	First Battle of Newbury.
1644	Second Battle of Newbury.
1653	Dr Sheaff founded free Grammar School.
1654	John Evelyn visited.
1668	Samuel Pepys visited.
1686	White Hart Inn mentioned.
1688	Meeting of William of Orange and James II Commissioners.
1733	Gate and rails at southern limit of town.
1740	Bridge Street made.
1744	Newbury–Marlborough Turnpike Acts.

1786	Third Town Hall built.
1788	First meeting to consider Western Canal.
1798	Western Canal opened to Hungerford.
1801	First Congregational Church built.
1805	Pond in High Street filled in.
1807	Old Wesleyan Chapel in Church Lane built.
1810	Kennet and Avon Canal fully opened.
1811	Enclosure Act.
1814	National School built.
1814-16	New Church of St Lawrence built.
1816	First bank in Hungerford.
1830-31	Reform Riots locally – Tannery windows smashed.
1832	Reform Bill passed – dinner given for 1,800 poor persons.
1836	Height of coaching era – 200 coaches weekly on Bath Road.
1837	Turnstiles erected in Little Church Lane.
1840	New Congregational Church built.
1842	Westfield House School established.
1845	Hungerford Gas Company registered.
1847	Railway opened to Hungerford terminus station.
1847	New workhouse opened off Cow Lane.
1848	By now only three coaches weekly on Bath Road.
1852	Kennet and Avon Canal bought by GWR.
1858	Night School established.
1862	Railway extended west to Devizes.
1863	Little Church Lane turnstile replaced by posts.
1864	Primitive Methodist Chapel built.
1868	St Saviours Church built.
1869	Wesleyan Chapel built.
1870	New Town Hall and Corn Exchange built.
1874	Railway converted to standard gauge.
1877	Last year canal made a profit.
1879	Restoration of St Lawrences completed.
1884	Old Grammar School in Croft closed.
1891	First steam fire engine.
1892	First fire station built in Charnham Street.
1894	Boundary changes bringing Charnham Street into Hungerford.
1896	Second railway bridge over High Street.
1899	St John's Mission Hall built.
1900	Church House built.
1901	Church House club formed.
1903	Water Works company formed.
1907	School added to Primitive Methodist Chapel.
1908	Formation of Town & Manor Charity, under Charity Commissioners.
1909	New drainage scheme.
1910	New steam fire engine.
1910	New 'council' school built in Fairview Road.
1910	Visit of King George V to Chilton.

1914	Post Office built.
1915	180 Company A.S.C., M.T. stationed in Hungerford.
1920	Widening of Bridge Street: Dedication of War Memorial.
1921	Sports ground opened in The Croft.
1924	Motorised fire engine 'John of Gaunt'.
1944	General Eisenhower addressed American troops on Common.
1948	George VI and Queen Elizabeth passed through Hungerford.
1952	Queen Elizabeth II and Prince Philip passed through the town.
1960	Fire destroyed James Mill.
1963	John of Gaunt Secondary School opened.
1964	Swimming pool opened.
1964	Railway station demolished.
1966	Third railway bridge over High Street.
1967	Library opened in Church Street.
1968	New fire station in Church Street built.
1970	Steam Fairs on the Common in aid of Corn Exchange restoration.
1971	Railway accident demolished signal box.
1971	M4 Motorway opened.
1974	Local government re-organization: first Mayor of Hungerford.
1974	Re-opening of Kennet and Avon Canal to Hungerford.
1978	New bells hung in St Lawrence's Church.
1981	Hungerford twinned with Ligueil.

Further Reading

The Story of Hungerford in Berkshire, Rev. W. H. Summers; 1926.

An Historical Sketch of the Town of Hungerford, Walter Money; 1894.

Chapter 1   Archeological Excavations in Littlecote Park, Wiltshire, B. Walters; 1978.
Historic Towns in Berkshire – an Archeological Appraisal, G. Astill; 1978.

Chapter 2   The Story of an Ancient Fishery, E. L. Davis; 1978.

Chapter 3   The 1st and 2nd Battles of Newbury and the Siege of Donnington Castle, Walter Money; 1884.
History of England from the Accession of James II, Lord Macaulay; 1881.
The Great Civil War – A Military History, A. H. Burne; 1959.

Chapter 4   The Mail Coach Men, Vale; 1960.
And So To Bath, Cecil Roberts; 1940.
Directory of Stage Coach Services 1836, Alan Bates, David and Charles; 1969.

Chapter 5   The Kennet & Avon Canal – an Illustrated History, Kenneth Clew; 1967.
The Story of the Parish Church of St. Lawrence, Hungerford, Rev. Finch, Wardley-King and Tagg; 1967.

Chapter 6   Historical Record of 180 Coy R.A.S.C., M.T., G. Lipscombe; 1919.

Index